Terry Gould

LEARNING AND PLAYING
OUTDOORS

How to plan and create an
inspiring outdoor environment

Published 2014 by Featherstone Education
Bloomsbury Publishing Plc
50 Bedford Square, London, WC1B 3DP
www.bloomsbury.com

ISBN 978-1-4081-9317-4

A CIP catalogue for this book is available from the British Library.

Printed and bound in India by Replika Press Pvt. Ltd

10 9 8 7 6 5 4 3 2 1

This book is produced using paper that is made from wood grown in
managed, sustainable forests. It is natural, renewable and recyclable.
The logging and manufacturing process conform to the environmental
regulations of the country of origin.

To see our full range of titles visit www.bloomsbury.com

Thank you to all the children and practitioners whose images appear in this
book with special mention to: St Margaret Ward RC Primary, Sale Cheshire;
Cosy, Derby; Medlock Primary School, Manchester; Kids Unlimited Group (now
Bright Horizons); St James CE Primary, Manchester; Old Hall Drive Primary,
Manchester; Ringway Primary School, Manchester; Alma Park Primary School,
Manchester; Acorn Childcare Ltd, Milton Keynes and the London Early Years
Foundation, London.

Contents

The importance of high quality outdoor learning

From the earliest days of the twentieth century, some of the great educators like Margaret McMillan have understood the need for children to be engaged in learning outdoors.

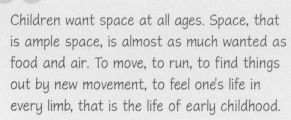

> Children want space at all ages. Space, that is ample space, is almost as much wanted as food and air. To move, to run, to find things out by new movement, to feel one's life in every limb, that is the life of early childhood.
>
> Margaret McMillan (1930)

Lesley Staggs more recently recognised the challenges of outdoor play in the twenty–first century when she raised the important notion that outdoor play is not an optional extra but a necessary entitlement.

> Lack of adequate outdoor play is a challenge for many...Inadequate provision cannot be accepted as permanent...By ensuring all staff and governors understand that the outdoor classroom is as key to the delivery of the Foundation Stage Curriculum as books and pencils, they are less likely to see the investment needed as an optional extra.
>
> Lesley Staggs, Conference keynote Manchester (2001)

In 2008 Ofsted confirmed that:

> When planned and implemented well, learning outside the classroom contributes significantly to raising standards and improving pupils' PSE development.
> Ofsted (2008)

The importance of outdoor learning was reinforced by the introduction of the Early Years Foundation Stage (EYFS) in 2007 and the revised framework in 2012. Sadly, the revised EYFS guidance offers only a minimal level of advice on how to provide an enabling environment outdoors and today's practitioners both need and deserve more than this.

All of today's children need the motivation and inspiration that can only be provided through the great outdoors. Indeed, for many vulnerable children learning and playing outdoors can have a huge impact on their emotional well-being and development.

All three of the newly named prime areas of development in the revised EYFS, which are identified as being essential for children, can be provided outdoors in 'bucketfuls'.

- **Communication and Language**

- **Physical Development**

- **Personal, Social and Emotional Development**

Outdoor play is here to stay and under the current framework is an entitlement for all children. There can be no doubt that young children need it like the very air they breathe. It is vital that we provide an enabling environment outdoors that inspires children's sense of exploration, discovery, awe and wonder.

Our task as EYFS practitioners is to ensure that we make this into a reality by providing the highest quality outdoor provision possible, and this includes ensuring our children have access to as wide a range of natural materials and experiences as possible. It is hoped that this book will help to support and inspire you in this mission.

'Let's get them outdoors'–
meeting the requirements of the revised EYFS

Practitioners are now required to plan a challenging and enjoyable experience for each child in all of the areas of learning and development. Under the revised EYFS framework (2012), children continue to have a statutory entitlement to daily, quality, outdoor learning. Part of this entitlement is access to a wide range and variety of stimulating outdoor experiences. The benefits to children of engaging in stimulating activities outdoors is well documented and it is now widely accepted, among settings, that when they provide outdoor learning it is on the understanding that:

- **there is benefit in being outdoors for babies, toddlers, nursery and reception stage children**

- **children need space and time outdoors where they can investigate, explore and repeat experiences**

- **children need to be physically active and nowhere is this more possible than outdoors.**

With the increased emphasis on welfare and safeguarding it is necessary under the revised Framework to consider health, safety and security issues outdoors. This will involve practitioners undertaking risk assessments (see page 57) and ensuring that these will reduce the risks, but is not about 'wrapping children up in cotton wool' so much that there are unnecessary barriers preventing them from having challenging and rich learning experiences.

As young children learn through using their senses, the whole EYFS staff team must make sure that there is an appropriate level of sensory stimulation outdoors. This has implications for what is provided and for the role of the adult outdoors. It has long been identified that the role of the EYFS practitioner is key to the success of all outdoor provision. The practitioner should observe, assess, guide and support children outdoors in the same way as they would indoors.

Unless you already have a suitably developed space/s outdoors to meet the revised EYFS requirements then it may be that you require significant funding to be made available, so as to turn some outdoor spaces into the inspiring areas they need to be – spaces which support all seven areas of learning.

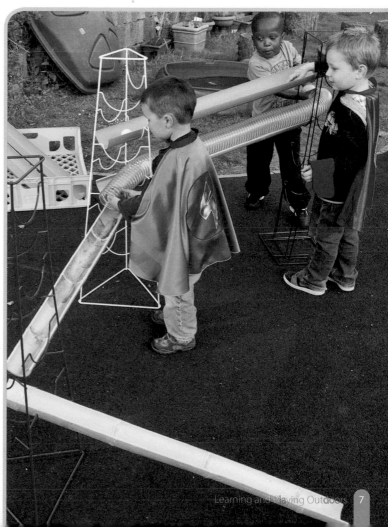

Fixed or portable provision

One aspect of outdoor spaces that often appears to elude some practitioners is the fact that there should to be an appropriate balance between fixed and portable equipment and resources.

★ **Fixed equipment should be as open ended as possible and help to define the purpose and possibilities of the space.**

★ **Portable resources are like 'the bricks in the mortar' that help to extend but also hold the thing together.**

One of the big bonuses with fixed equipment is that it does not take time to set up and put away. The downside can be the lack of flexibility that some fixed equipment offers.

Whatever the nature of the outdoor space you have within your provision it has the potential to be developed and further improved. Any development of an outdoor area is likely to be defined and determined by what the children who attend the setting/ school need to experience and learn. Hence a good starting point is current and previous data (both qualitative and quantitative), as this will help to identify what children at the school/setting need most. This will help to form the basis of the 'educational programme' (EYFS 2012) that you will offer them.

The development of any outdoor space/s is often best approached as a three part process:

(i) Things you can do immediately or thereabouts that will not cost a lot of money or take a lot of time.

(ii) Things that can be done within a few weeks/months and may cost a small amount of money.

(iii) Things that will need to be undertaken in the longer term due to the time and cost implications, and planned through the school/setting development plan.

Training and development

Developments in outdoor provision should be supported by ongoing training and development for all practitioners, because to deliver the current EYFS requirements outdoors the workforce will need to continuously improve and demonstrate their:

◆ **understanding of the individual and the diverse ways children learn and develop**

◆ **practice in meeting all children's needs, learning styles and interests**

◆ **work with parents, carers and the wider community**

◆ **knowledge and understanding of the educational programme offered in order to actively support and extend children's learning in and across all areas and aspects of learning**

◆ **ability to work with other professionals within and beyond the setting.**

The revised EYFS guidance framework covers three areas:

■ **learning and development**

■ **assessment**

■ **safeguarding and welfare.**

Each of these has strong links to outdoor provision. Children can learn on a larger scale outdoors and there are many things outdoor spaces offer which cannot be replicated indoors.

Outdoors should always provide children with opportunities which are:

◆ **bigger**

◆ **bolder**

◆ **messier and noisier.**

As an example of this point is that there is little value or purpose in taking the small wooden building bricks outside!

The weather and seasons alone ensure that children experience a range and variety of conditions and situations outdoors, which can range from the smell, touch and vision of freshly mown grass to that of feeling the cold, to the exhilarating sense of the first snowfall and then making snowballs or a snow person.

There is much outdoors that supports the children sensory development through the use of their senses and involving their hands. As Kranowitz (2005) reminds us:

> the tactile system, or sense of touch, plays a major part in determining physical, mental and emotional human behaviour.
>
> Kranowitz (2005)

Tactile experience in the child's earliest years as they explore and investigate materials and sounds and copy others is critically important to their development. Receptors in the child's skin capture a wide range of stimulating sensations such as vibrations, stretch, movement, temperature, and of course, pain. Children will get a wider range and variety of tactile experiences outdoors than they will ever do indoors as they feel the wind in their hair, the sun warming their bodies as well as the different surface textures they walk on from grass to concrete and rubberised surface to soil.

Chapter 2

Good practice in outdoor provision

Some of the best 'resources' for young children outdoors are tuned in, enthusiastic practitioners and other children. Practitioners can make or break the quality and nature of outdoor experiences for children. Practitioners who understand child development are essential as they will recognise and know that when babies and very young children who are outdoors appear to be doing little or nothing, they are in fact busy making sense of the world.

Knowledgeable and experienced practitioners can help children to get the most from outdoors and they are the key to introducing children to exciting experiences. Children need a breadth and variety of experiences outdoors which can only be offered where the value and nature of high quality provision and practice is fully understood by all staff.

Practitioners need to be fully committed to being outdoors with children, and all settings should ensure that they make their philosophy on outdoor learning clear during the recruitment and induction process.

Children need four things in abundance outdoors:

1. **Time to engage**

2. **Space to engage in**

3. **Support for their emotional well-being**

4. **A secure environment that is safe but offers interest and suitable age-appropriate challenges.**

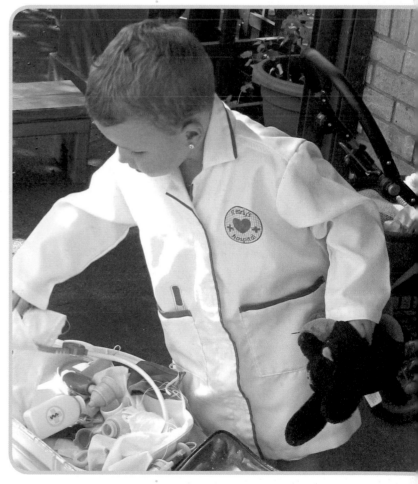

Good practice in the outdoor environment is always better where it provides a balance between fixed and portable equipment and resources. As previously identified, where items are fixed these need to be as open–ended as possible. Portable resources and equipment will need to be stimulating and interesting and offer an open ended variety of uses. Such portable items can support fixed equipment and resources as well as offering new experiences and dimensions.

The resources and equipment provided outdoors should be determined by:

★ **what the children need to support their learning and development across all seven areas of learning**

★ **where children are up to in their learning and development (stages)**

★ **what interests and inspires the children.**

Hence when developing a new area, or reviewing an existing outdoor area, the past data on the progress and development of children can be a vital tool to consider. No two settings will ever have exactly the same resources and equipment as the children's needs and interests will be different, as will the nature and size of the space available outdoors. Although some similarities will exist there will be equally as many differences to consider.

Planning your provision

When people ask me 'What should I provide outdoors?', the advice I always give is that the first consideration should be the experiences the children need – followed by the resources that the children will then require to engage with these experiences.

On a practical basis, I am including here a list of some tried and tested good portable resources that you may wish to consider including in your outdoor setting:

- ✓ watering cans – **different sizes**
- ✓ **wheelbarrows** – child sizes
- ✓ **brushes and brooms** – range and variety
- ✓ **natural materials such as large pebbles and shells**
- ✓ **guttering, tubes, pipes and funnels**
- ✓ **lengths of hosepipe**
- ✓ **gardening tools** – long and short handled
- ✓ **metal pots and pans**
- ✓ **suitcases, rucksacks and baskets**
- ✓ **range of sizes of tyres**

- ✓ **wood pieces and logs**
- ✓ **ropes of different lengths** (not nylon)
- ✓ **joining materials such as pegs, tape, string and ribbons**
- ✓ **milk and bakery trays**
- ✓ **rainwear, Wellington boots, umbrellas**
- ✓ **jumbo chalk**
- ✓ **blankets and sheets**
- ✓ **cardboard boxes**
- ✓ **fabric and ribbons**
- ✓ **clothes horse/s**

These resources, you will note, are open-ended and hence can offer and support a wide range of experiences. With more portable resources comes a requirement for more storage, so this needs thinking about carefully or it can soon become an issue.

It is critically important that there is the right ethos towards outside play in the setting/school. This will ensure that all staff recognise the commitment the setting places on learning outdoors. It will also ensure that children are given access to the outdoor space as through continuous free flow play provision between indoors and outdoors. In my time I have seen some great outdoor environments created which later have lapsed into lack of use due to the ethos not being retained when a new leader takes over. Most often this has been in schools but also in some children's centres and day care settings. Children need outdoor experiences and the revised EYFS re-affirms that it is their entitlement.

Good practice outdoors will include two key elements:

★ **the physical environment created**

★ **the practitioners involved.**

These will be underpinned by good maintenance of the space and daily accessibility for all children.

Establishing stage–appropriate outdoor provision

How you physically design, develop and set up your outdoor area will depend on the size and nature of the space and the needs of your children. If you are creating new outdoor provision, make sure that you set aside an appropriate level of budget for developing this. Even if you don't have a large amount of space it is still possible to create exciting learning opportunities for children. Whatever the size of the space and whether you are developing new or existing provision there are aspects that you will need to consider.

Getting started

You will need to think about some essential aspects from the start including these.

Establishing zones

Establishing outdoor zones is simply a way of dividing up the space so that while everything can flow easily some areas/activities don't interfere with others. How you decide on these zones will depend on the ages/stages of children who will be using the area.

→ **Start by thinking about what the needs of the children are and what experiences you want them to have outdoors.**

→ **Consider access to the outside and the practicality of how children can and will engage with what you set up.**

→ **Think about how you will ensure appropriate levels of shade and shelter for children.**

→ **Reflect on storage – how you store equipment and resources will impact on what you provide. You might decide a purpose-built shed or container is the answer.**

→ **Remember zones need to be flexible to allow for changes in the children's needs and interests as they develop/grow older.**

Surfaces

■ These can be level, sloped, raised or sunken and may include tunnels to provide opportunities for the children to roll, crawl, walk and run.

■ Different surfaces can facilitate different experiences and it is wise to think these through carefully, including reflecting on drainage, remembering that there can be major cost implications in any hard landscaping work that may be required.

■ A variety of surfacing is always best. Rubber surfacing is a popular choice but a dominance of this may inhibit some experiences.

Shade and shelter

◆ This can be open-ended, you will need different shelters including child-sized gazebos of wooded structure.

◆ Partial shading through planted trees or the canopy of the building itself.

◆ Protective clothing including umbrellas rainwear suits, Wellington boots, sunglasses, long sleeved T-shirts and so on.

Meeting the needs of babies outdoors

> The thirst for understanding springs from the child's deepest emotional needs.
>
> Isaacs S. (1932)

Rather than merely trying to take some of the indoors outside, it is most important for babies in their first year of life that their need is met to experience the outdoors first hand in all its glory, and through this they can begin to realise the unique nature of the outdoors environment.

There are a vast range of differences between the indoors and outdoors environment and it is vital that young children's experiences capture this. Babies can tune in very quickly to the differences between outdoors and indoors. After their basic fascination with other human beings, babies have a growing interest in objects around them. This innate interest is supported through an awareness of the properties of these objects – what they do and how they behave when touched or moved. Some of the most interesting and useful objects to surround babies with are natural ones such as stones, wood, grass, soil etc. as well as those from the human domestic world such as domestic tools and utensils including pots, pans, spoons etc. Watching how small children manipulate these materials and objects and the close attention they give to them reinforces our understanding of the intensity of their engagement and exploration.

The natural world can provide a huge array of appropriate, exploratory, highly sensory play-based learning opportunities for babies. Babies' attention is often quickly drawn to the smallest details such as the delicacy of a flower or leaf, the patterns in pieces of cut wood, the texture of bark on a tree and how sand and water can be explored.

Practitioners need to allow babies time to explore all of these things in their own time and at their own pace. These will be deeply significant, complex and important experiences for the very young baby that allow them to develop their appreciation and understanding of the world around them, alongside an innate satisfaction.

Meeting the needs of babies outdoors (contd.)

For babies, engagement with natural materials is excellent for supporting:

- **sensory development**

- **motor development**

- **cognitive development.**

Your own observations of babies engaging and interacting in such ways will allow you to reflect on how much each of our very youngest children need nature and how much they have this inborn affinity with it. The outdoors provides for babies what the indoors cannot. To gain a balanced perspective of the world around them it is important that babies spend plenty of time outdoors. This has implications for good practice in settings.

When babies move to the outdoors they very quickly pick up on the contrasting sensations of the seasonal and weather elements on their faces and bodies. This contrast alerts the baby's brain and helps to focus his/her attention. The practitioner, by holding the baby securely and being attentive to their needs/interests, offers the conditions which enable the baby to activate their inborn exploration systems. Because of their natural affinity and fascination with the outside world, one of the easiest ways to settle a young baby is to take them to a window to look outside — or better still, take them outside.

When outdoors, babies use sight, touch, taste, smell, sound and movement to explore the world around them and make sense of it. Very young babies up to around six to nine months respond to people and situations with their whole bodies as they respond to the immediate environment around them.

What matters to babies outdoors is things that they find interesting — and babies focus for much longer on things to which their interest is naturally drawn. They need to be taken out to the park, the streets and to the shops, as well as to any attached outdoor spaces, as these offer interesting and contrasting experiences for them. Frequent and repeated short trips and walks into the community and locality are invaluable for babies.

> Revisiting the same places many times is more valuable than trips to different places every time.
>
> Gould T. (2012)

The outdoor world changes constantly, and while some features are the same, others are not. This can be very supportive of babies' perception, comprehension and physical skills, which develop and change so quickly in a familiar outdoor landscape that is ever changing and presents new opportunities for babies to see, hear and smell different things and opportunities to learn about these. What the child sees, hears and smells on a walk in the early part of spring will be vastly different in the heart of the summer, and again to that in the autumn or winter.

Local environments provide rich and stimulating places to spend time where practitioners can observe and then respond to the baby's agenda. Trips out, while valuable in their own right, are a great way to supplement the limitations of a small outdoor space and very young children will become confident and comfortable exploring places they visit regularly and enjoy.

Practitioners need to observe what babies are attracted to outdoors as this will tell them a great deal about what is going on in the child's mind. Even very young babies are already competent in observing and responding to what is immediately around them. All babies should be taken outdoors on a daily basis and supported in experiencing different temperatures and weather conditions including sun, rain, wind and snow.

Older babies, between nine and 18 months, become more intentional in their exploration outdoors. Their increasing levels of mobility and developing levels of language enable them to interact more with the environment on a more independent level. At this stage they begin to enjoy observing and interacting with other children around them.

Meeting the needs of toddlers outdoors

> Young children take in information about
> the external world by physically and bodily-
> interacting with it, and build understanding by
> moving through it and manipulating it.
> White J. (2008)

Just as with babies, toddlers continue to have a strong affinity with the natural world and enjoy being outdoors where they can experience it. Daily opportunities to be outdoors for toddlers remain an essential part of provision in meeting their needs. As children start to walk they are enabled to explore and investigate under their own steam and become much less reliant on practitioners.

It is important that practitioners recognise and respond to the fact that young children at the toddler stage (18 months to 24 months):

- **still learn predominantly through their senses and physical experiences**

- **seek out natural materials which they can combine together, such as sand or soil and water, and begin to transport items from one place to another.**

For the toddler, the outdoor space is very special as it offers them something different from the indoor space.

This can include:

* ✶ natural light, fresh air, sunshine and greater levels of oxygen

* ✶ more space and freedom to move on a range of different surfaces

* ✶ a much wider range of interesting stimuli

* ✶ daily changes to be experienced brought on by the weather and the seasons

* ✶ direct physical and emotional contact with the natural world

* ✶ a different but wider space to watch and interact with people and build up relationships.

The toddler is innately strongly driven to explore and will be hugely disadvantaged if he/she is restricted only to the indoors to do this. Not only will it affect the levels of their language development but also their emotional well-being.

Toddlers need provision outdoors that includes:

* ◆ natural materials including sand, water, soil and mud

* ◆ space to run and move

* ◆ a variety of surfaces on which to walk and run

* ◆ an adventure area where they can climb crawl and balance

* ◆ a place to engage in imaginative role play

* ◆ sensory stimulation

* ◆ places to grow and care for plants and vegetables

* ◆ place to mark–make.

Meeting the needs of two year olds and pre-school children outdoors

> Children play, grow and feel the world around them.
>
> Keeler R. (2008)

While all young children need daily outdoor play and learning, this is particularly important for children aged two and above as they are becoming increasingly mobile and are more able to move around quickly, safely and independently. They have an innate thirst to explore and investigate, to move, to touch, to breathe and to be outdoors — and the practitioner must ensure their healthy development and well-being which is inescapably somehow tied up with the outdoors. Independent and co-operative play skills are developing at this age and children need a wide range of real experiences which are purposeful, relevant and meaningful to them.

Movement continues to be important for this stage of development and these children need even more space to run and move than the toddler. Movement experiences that children have outdoors, on a bigger scale than indoors, will help them to develop essential structures within the brain and nervous systems which also serve to support cognitive and physical outcomes. All of this will ensure an environment where emotional well-being and mental well-being are supported and where self-esteem and positive self-image continue to be fostered.

As they grow and develop, children need a wide and varied range of opportunities. They need to be able to set themselves challenges and learn what it means to keep themselves safe and healthy. A rich environment outdoors which offers such physical and cognitive experiences will provide an endless series of opportunities for play and talk, exploration and discovery to take place. All of this will enable new experiences and developing concepts to be enhanced, processed and understood.

To meet children's needs at this stage, adults need to tune in to what is happening in their play and exploration and then use this to plan for the next steps in their learning.

The two year old/pre-school child needs outdoor spaces which challenge them and allow them time and space to engage in sustained involvement in a wide range of activities. The outdoor space needs to be recognised as an important part of what is on offer and provide opportunities to develop in all seven areas of learning and development. Movement stimulates the young child's brain and is an essential element outdoors.

Two to three year olds need provision outdoors that engages with their interests and meets their growing needs. This should include:

- ✓ **space to construct and deconstruct – to build and to knock down**

- ✓ **space to engage with wheeled toys**

- ✓ **natural materials including sand, water, soil and mud**

- ✓ **space to run and move, play ball games and engage in other activities such as parachute games**

- ✓ **a variety of surfaces on which to walk and run**

- ✓ **adventure spaces where they can climb, swing, crawl and balance**

- ✓ **a place to engage in imaginative role play**

- ✓ **a natural space with trees, shrubs and grass**

- ✓ **sensory stimulation space/s**

- ✓ **places to grow and care for plants and vegetables**

- ✓ **place to paint, draw and mark make and be creative**

- ✓ **place to investigate minibeasts.**

Meeting the needs of children in nursery and reception classes outdoors

If we don't capture the potential of the outdoors we are missing the point — missing the huge capacity of the outdoors to help young children to thrive and grow.

White J. (2009)

The key to outdoor learning at this stage is providing an environment where high quality continuous provision is available through free flow between indoors and outdoors.

Three to five year olds need provision outdoors that includes:

→ **space to engage in structured ways with wheeled toys**

→ **space to engage with natural materials including sand, water, soil and mud**

→ **space to run and move, play ball games and engage in other activities such as parachute games**

→ **space to engage in 'performing arts'**

→ **space to sit and be quieter and/or to engage in less boisterous and quieter activities**

→ **a variety of surfaces on which to walk and run**

→ **space where they can climb, swing, crawl and balance**

→ **specific themed space/spaces to engage in imaginative role play**

→ **natural space/s with trees, shrubs and grass**

→ **sensory stimulation area**

→ **places to grow and care for plants and vegetables**

→ **place/s to paint, draw and write**

→ **space which supports them being creative**

→ **spaces to explore and investigate including minibeasts.**

Meeting the needs of Year 1 children outdoors

 The best outdoor provision takes place when there is an approach to outdoor learning that considers experiences rather than equipment and in this way places the child at the centre of the provision being made.

DfES (2007)

Nowhere is the above quote more relevant than with children in Year 1. These children have usually spent two years in a nursery and a reception class and they will have had access to the outdoors on a daily basis – often through continuous free flow provision. Now, on moving into Year 1 they very often only get outdoor play at school playtimes or dinner times. The increased use of school grounds for small groups and the use of a fenced, attached space to the Year 1 classroom can provide the answer to ensuring continuity and progression into Year 1.

The fenced off area doesn't have to be large – 6 metres by 4 metres as a minimum would suffice although an area much bigger than this would be better. The case study in Chapter 6 on a Year 1 classroom developing an outdoor area is a useful one to focus on relating to this (page 50).

Outdoor provision in Year 1 should focus on the experiences children need and this may be determined by looking at existing data of achievement and observations of the children as learners.

Ideally the areas to develop outside would include:

* ★ **imaginative play area**

* ★ **writing/drawing area**

* ★ **seating/gathering area**

* ★ **larger flexible area for mathematical games and other activities such as large scale water play with gutters and pipes**

* ★ **outdoor sand pit area**

* ★ **performing arts area.**

If your outside space is particularly small you can rotate these areas within the space available. The experiences in each of these areas can be supported by outdoor resource boxes. What is developed and provided outdoors in Year 1 will very much depend on the space and funding available, linked closely to the children's identified learning needs.

Chapter 4
Observation, assessment and
planning outdoors

Observation, assessment and planning outdoors

Observation outdoors describes the process of watching, listening and taking notes. Effective teaching and learning outdoors cannot take place without this process being of a consistently good quality.

There must be opportunities provided for children to engage in activities they choose, plan and initiate themselves, as well as those planned and led by practitioners. It is increasingly recognised that activities, freely chosen, can often provide the best opportunities for children to demonstrate what they know and can do, as well as to extend their thinking.

The observation, assessment and planning cycle is covered in the EYFS non-statutory guidance Development Matters (2012). In all EYFS settings/schools this should be supported by staff training which will ensure that all staff:

★ **have good observation skills**

★ **understand and implement assessment for learning**

★ **are able to make sound, accurate assessments from observations**

★ **work in consistent way/s.**

All this will be within a context that what they do is manageable and is not excessive or unworkable in terms of time spent.

Manager, leaders and practitioners should reflect on the following:

◆ **observation outdoors should always be seen as a key part of a practitioner's daily role**

◆ **the benefits of involving parents in observations of their child at home**

◆ **strategies to help with observations**

◆ **the fact that EYFS experiences should build on existing skills and knowledge and be matched appropriately to children's needs and levels of competence**

◆ **how observations link to the characteristics of effective learning**

◆ **the difference between formative and summative assessments**

◆ **the importance of linking observations to planning.**

Where staff are new to the EYFS or relatively inexperienced, the management-led supervision process should ensure that their needs receive due levels of support. All staff should be supported in their understanding that the more they know about the child, the better able they will be to effectively support subsequent learning.

It is highly important that practitioners recognise that only a few of the many observations they make of children ever need to be written down. It comes down to the fact that only those which are significant should be recorded in writing, the rest just become mental notes. For some staff understanding what is significant may be an aspect with which they will need support.

How we use observations made outdoors is critically important. To be best utilised, practitioners need to gather observations that are:

● **planned**

● **spontaneous.**

These should then be used to inform planning and provision by:

◾ **building on what children already know and can do**

◾ **providing differentiation for children's different starting points**

◾ **providing relevant and appropriate experiences that match children's learning and development needs**

◾ **support and extend children's confidence, skills, knowledge and understanding**

◾ **sharing and discussing with parents/carers to involve them in the assessment process.**

To maximise opportunities to gather information through observation there needs to be a suitably challenging and supportive outdoor environment that is continuously enhanced to meet children's indentified needs.

In less than high quality provision, poor quality outdoor observations often have a poor outdoor environment as a limiting factor. There are less likely to be significant aspects to record where provision is less than required and where the provision does not inspire children to become engaged.

Practitioners should gather evidence on children's achievements outdoors throughout their EYFS years and use this to chart their progress and development.

This should include:

★ Participant observations where the practitioners engage in play/activity with the child/ren.

★ Participant observations where the practitioner is involved in adult-led, planned activities.

★ Incidental observations where the practitioner notices something which is significant in what the child is engaging in.

★ Planned or focused observations where the practitioner stands back to observe the child/ren in independent play-based activities.

★ Conversations with children or one-to-one chats, as well as informal conversations and discussions.

★ Utilising additional information from parents on their child at home.

★ Samples of things children produce such as photos of models and other creative work.

★ Photos of children carrying out an activity which show the learning process in which they are engaged.

★ Evidence from other professionals such as speech and language therapists, special support assistants, physiotherapists, bilingual assistants etc.

★ Evidence of learning and development from other settings/ providers that the child attends such as playgroup, childminder, after school club etc.

Chapter 5
The role of the adult outdoors
Including partnership with parents

Chapter 5

Chapter 5
The role of the adult outdoors –
including partnership with parents

The role of the adult outdoors – including partnership with parents

Effective practice indoors and outdoors requires committed, enthusiastic and reflective practitioners with a depth of knowledge, skills and understanding. They are a key component of any EYFS enabling environment.

The role of the adult outdoors, including the interactions between adults and children, is vital. Some key aspects of this role include that practitioners:

◆ **are aware of those children who may need encouragement**

◆ **observe children and use this to plan and evaluate rich and stimulating outdoor learning activities based on an understanding of how children learn and develop – including the next steps for individual children's learning**

◆ **ensure a relevant educational programme which covers all seven areas of learning**

◆ **set up challenging situations for children to explore and investigate**

◆ **intervene and extend play appropriately**

◆ **act as a role model**

◆ **act as a play leader**

◆ **extend and develop children's language, communication and thinking skills**

◆ **help to raise children's awareness of health and safety issues**

◆ **ensure the outdoor area is safe, secure and hazard free while remaining challenging**

◆ **promote and support child-initiated and independent learning**

◆ **respond appropriately to children's interests, patterns of behaviour, and cultural diversity.**

For children to be able to access outdoor learning independently in sustained ways, they need to know and understand the associated systems and routines. This will include knowing where and how to access their own coats and boots and how to store these. Support must also be in place for children to be outside in all weathers by providing additional suitable clothing as well as shade and shelter.

Chapter 5
The role of the adult outdoors-
including partnership with parents

Planning should consider the educational programme needed by the children. This will cover three main considerations, so as to ensure appropriate breadth and balance across all seven areas of learning:

- **resources**

- **activities**

- **experiences.**

Practitioners outdoors can effectively use the above to support children by creating and developing an exciting and stimulating space which meets their learning needs and builds on their developing knowledge, skills and interests. You can welcome and even enjoy the increased levels of noise created outdoors as children explore the freedom that the outdoor space and fresh air provide. You can join in or play alongside them and introduce new ideas to them while skilfully introducing language and new skills. It is often the case that you will discover a completely different side to the child than that displayed indoors, especially those who remain quiet and passive indoors.

The quality of the interactions between practitioners and children outdoors is central to higher order functioning (Wilshaw 2013, Vygotsky 1978, Wells 1987). Such higher level functioning involves children thinking through and reflecting on what they are doing and working to problem-solve. To develop intellectual control requires higher order thinking and is characterised by:

- ★ **use of logic**

- ★ **perseverance**

- ★ **concentrated thinking.**

When planning, staff will need to think about the needs of the children and use this to consider how best to set up outdoors for the day ahead. The staff role is key and involves bringing the children, the environment and the educational programme together. Quality provision, through effective planning and evaluation, does not occur without teams working together. Indoor and outdoor planning should be seen as one and not be completed on two separate sheets. Fixed equipment outdoors should be seen as far as possible as flexible/open ended resources. The provision outdoors therefore cannot be seen as static but rather as an ever-changing space which keeps pace with children's growing needs and interests.

Chapter 5
The role of the adult outdoors-
including partnership with parents

Partnership with parents

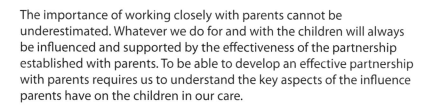

> Parents, carers and the wider family are the main providers of love, care and support for children and young people and therefore have the most significant contribution to make in helping children to achieve the five outcomes.
>
> *Every Child Matters* (2005)

The importance of working closely with parents cannot be underestimated. Whatever we do for and with the children will always be influenced and supported by the effectiveness of the partnership established with parents. To be able to develop an effective partnership with parents requires us to understand the key aspects of the influence parents have on the children in our care.

Parents need to have a clear understanding of what their children are learning when they are outdoors. Frequent updates of children's progress is an important part of this, some of which will be informal, while other parts will comprise the regular three times a year formal meeting. It is always useful to try to engage with parents to provide them with the opportunity to share any special expertise or interests in the outdoors which they have and to be involved at a level with which they are comfortable.

We need to ensure that not only are parents supported by us, but that they *feel* they are supported by us! To do this we can help them to:

→ **value the provision we offer their child outdoors**

→ **support their child/ren learning outdoors at home and at the setting**

→ **keep their child safe outdoors**

→ **support their child's cognitive and physical development outdoors**

→ **support their child's emotional well-being outdoors.**

To achieve the above you will need to reassure parents about the importance of their role, and how any work is joint work for the benefit of their child and is a partnership in which each values and respects the other. We can do this though creating a framework for two-way communication and engagement with parents in which the key messages are channelled.

Chapter 5
The role of the adult outdoors-
including partnership with parents

Parents must be kept well informed of their child's progress and development and any identified needs transmitted both ways between home and the setting. Part of this will include how children engage with outdoor learning, their interests as well as their likes and dislikes outdoors. Giving parents the opportunity to read the observations made on their child outdoors will greatly help, as will their contributions of their child at home to the learning journey, compiled by the setting.

Before the child starts at your setting/school it is useful, if not essential, to provide parents with information on the nature, benefits and importance of outdoor learning your setting provides. At this point it should be stressed that within the EYFS quality outdoor learning is both statutory and the entitlement of every child.

The more we engage with parents about the benefits of outdoor learning the better their understanding of it is likely to be, including their understanding of the importance of it for their child. Not all parents will start with the same level of understanding as others and even the best informed parents will not have had your training. They will not therefore have developed your understanding of the value and benefits of outdoor learning. Your task is to ensure that all parents as far as possible enjoy a shared vision with your team, and become more knowledgeable and more enthusiastic the longer their child attends your setting.

Chapter 5
The role of the adult outdoors-
including partnership with parents

Chapter 5
The role of the adult outdoors-
including partnership with parents

The adult role is key to the success of outdoor play in all weathers

As practitioners who work in UK settings, we have to cope with ever–changing and sometimes fast–changing weather conditions. As a result, planning for outdoor play/provision needs to be flexible. When designing and developing the outdoor area, practitioners should take into account all the different ranges and combinations of weather, including wind, rain, snow, frost, sun and the extremes of hot and cold.

Whilst as adults we might get somewhat frustrated with the climate in which we work and the ensuing weather conditions, this is much less likely to be the case for children. They are more likely to be excited by weather conditions such as snow, hail stones, wind or rain. Shade and shelter in the outdoor environment are important in enabling children to take advantage of all types of weather. The outdoor environment needs to be protected as much as possible from the wind by fencing, walls, buildings, bushes and trees or a combination of these. It also needs to offer lots of protection from the sun through shade, offered by permanent and temporary structures.

Young children's understanding of the weather and seasons and other scientific concepts is relatively undeveloped. Teaching and learning outdoors in the EYFS needs to be more responsive to children's learning needs and adults need to be well prepared to support children learning outdoors, whatever the weather!

Chapter 5
The role of the adult outdoors-
including partnership with parents

Having ideas for planning that build on children's natural enthusiasm for windy, rainy or snowy days is one way of approaching things. Where resources are well organised in advance, such plans can easily be implemented when the need arises, and less 'adult friendly' weather rather than posing a problem instead becomes an opportunity for children to engage in enjoyable and meaningful learning outdoors. There is a well known Scandinavian saying which states that there is no such thing as bad weather, only unsuitable clothing!

The outdoor environment offers valuable learning opportunities for children at all times of the year and in all weathers, and all-weather outdoor resource boxes can be one way of being organised in advance. Such boxes might include a 'windy day box' or a 'rainy day box' along with appropriate shade and shelter resources and equipment. Children will often also want to be outdoors in sunny weather so shade and shelter is important particularly when the sun is strong.

Outdoors, the practitioner's main goals should include:

★ **To promote autonomous independent and peer play**

★ **To support focused pretend play**

★ **To provide time and space and support the duration of autonomous pretend play.**

Chapter 5
The role of the adult outdoors-
including partnership with parents

Quality preparation precedes quality play and explorations

These goals are more likely to happen in reality when the outdoor environment has been carefully prepared to support this aim and therefore provides a stage appropriate balance between fixed and portable resources. By providing some definition in the established areas outdoors for play and exploration, the practitioners will be providing protected space where children are able to initiate interactions, make discoveries and negotiate with others. Space that is defined gives children the opportunity for both parallel and social interactive play and provides a range of open resources that can help this to be maintained and developed.

Children need adults who will support and take their learning forwards. Adults who do this best use a range of interactive and other strategies to support children using the environment, including:

✓ Adding to the provision in line with children's needs and interests

✓ Acting as role models

✓ Initiating activities and experiences

✓ Demonstrating skills or sharing knowledge

✓ Acknowledging and articulating a child's interests, actions or feelings e.g. providing a running commentary or repeating back

✓ Sharing their own experiences in conversational style

✓ Scaffolding experiences for individual children

✓ Asking questions and posing problems

✓ Intervening when appropriate

✓ Encouraging children e.g. to explore or investigate

✓ Motivating and fostering interests which they observe ensure that all children access outdoor provision

✓ Being aware of those children who may need encouragement

✓ Planning rich and stimulating outdoor learning activities which are stage appropriate

✓ Planning and evaluating appropriate learning activities using their understanding of how children learn and develop

✓ Ensuring that the provision covers all the EYFS seven areas of learning

✓ Setting up challenging situations for children to explore and investigate

✓ Extending play appropriately

✓ Sharing information formally and informally with parents about their child's learning outdoors

Case studies

Case study 1

Private day nursery outdoors

The nursery has an outdoor area of approximate 40 metres by
20 metres and also a small additional, overgrown plot which they
have recently acquired which is an additional 6 metres by 15
metres.

The space was only partly used by the children and overall was
not seen as inspiring. It needed a lot of work to make it the kind of
place that was required for high quality outdoor provision.

After visiting several other outdoor areas and consulting
with children and parents, plans were drawn up with an EYFS
consultant based around the needs of children from three months
to five years.

They included:

- a young babies area specifically just for children up to nine months

- a space where children could dig

- a low level climbing and adventure area

- a grassed area with a small hillock

- a natural area that would attract butterflies and other wildlife

- a willow tunnel

- a performing arts area, made from decking

- a paved area for wheeled toys

- a large outdoor, inset sandpit

- a four-post system to create dens and structures with the children

- a growing area with level ground and raised beds

- two large boards fixed to the wall for children to draw and to paint on a larger scale

- a semi open, wooden-covered structure which could be used for variety of purposes

- a large wooded storage shed

- a small wild area with logs where grass is allowed to grow wild.

The fixed equipment and ground work put into place will be supplemented by specialist outdoor clothing and a range of portable resources many of which are stored and accessible through a range of resource boxes.

These plans were then put out to tender. Once the budget was agreed, plans were finalised and work was commenced during the early part of March. It took several weeks to complete but the outcome was fantastic. Outdoor provision is now a real strength of the setting. Parents are delighted with the changes made and a very recent Ofsted inspection highly commended the setting for its outdoor provision .

Case study 2

Primary school outdoors

The EYFS (nursery and reception classes) in the school already had an outdoor space, but this was shared between nursery and reception and was limited in size – although the outdoor grounds for the rest of the school were quite generous. It was decided that the nursery and reception classes both needed their own area directly attached, to meet the requirements of the revised EYFS, but set up in way that these could be joined if required for some of the sessions.

The reception class area was much smaller than that of the nursery and it was decided that the existing fencing to the enclosed, very small space outside the reception class would be taken 12 metres back into the school playground and a new fence erected. Bushes were planted to the front of the new fencing, in large raised beds. An area for large scale water play was created. A new large raised sandpit was also installed. Additionally, a small gathering space was created with a storyteller chair and mini raised benches (each for two children to share) set into the ground. The area was completed with a covered wooden structure where group times could be held. The space was already covered in tarmac and raised beds were added along one side to allow planting and growing to take place of plants, flowers and vegetable. A designated space for ball play and running was set up.

Although the children still have to share the large physical equipment in the nursery area (they do so each day for half an hour while nursery get ready for their dinnertime) they now have their own suitably-sized space which can be accessed directly from their classroom. This allows them to engage fully with their daily entitlement to outdoor play on continuous access basis. They also use the large school grounds at selected times.

Children's centre outdoors

The children's centre is a traditional building of single storey construction with a modern extension to the front. It has good access to the outdoor provision from all but one of the rooms. The outdoor space comprised one large area, mainly laid to grass, to the front side of the building and another area to the rear side. This latter space was mainly laid to grass and mostly comprised of a large hillock with a steep slope on one side which lead directly onto metal railings that separated it from a railway line. The ground to the rear side had very poor drainage and when it rained for any lengthy period quite severe flooding took place.

The nursery staff held a staff training day at a nearby outward bound site organised by the manager. This was led by an external consultant who was already familiar with the setting. Initial discussion took place as to what the bland and uninteresting space could be like and outline plans were drawn up. It was decided that the rear area would be designated as the baby and toddler space. The large hillock with its steep slope was to be greatly lowered and soft bushes planted in front of the metal fence, screening if off and helping to soften the landscape.

The small flagged area was extended through the digging up of some of the grass and a soft surface area installed. Large mirrors were placed strategically in line close to the flagged and adjacent soft surface area creating a mirrored walkway. A range of bushes were planted including: Potentilla, Pieris/Forest Flame, Weiglea and Choisiya, Buddleia and Bamboo, along with a few small trees including: Sorbus/ Whitebeam, Silver Birch and a Cornus Florida Daybreak.

What a difference this has now made to the provision for the children — and of course it has impacted on improved outcomes and, for some of the boys in particular, significant gains were noted.

Primary school Year 1 outdoors

The Year 1 teacher wanted to be able to offer her children outdoor provision. Her classroom overlooked a small enclosed courtyard but there was no direct access to the outdoors, only two windows which looked onto the courtyard. It was agreed with the head that one of the windows could be opened out to provide a doorway access to the area, and this work was undertaken during the spring school holidays. The new outdoor classroom space was approximately 8 metres by 5 metres and already block paved with small birch trees planted to one side.

The Year 1 data over the past three years was looked at to identify the children's needs, and from this it was evident that mathematics, speaking and listening and writing were the main areas requiring more support. The children's ideas were also sought as to what experiences they would like outdoors. Among the things they fed back that they would like was a role play area, space to sit and read and talk, a place for ball games and 'somewhere to draw and write'.

From this an outline of the area was developed to include:

◆ **an outdoor role play area in one corner**

◆ **seating/gathering area seating around the tree**

◆ **larger flexible space for mathematical games and other activities such as large scale water play with gutters and pipes**

◆ **large chalking board, fixed to one wall**

◆ **a giant outdoor sandpit**

◆ **a covered workshop area**

◆ **a small performing arts stage.**

After obtaining quotes for the work, a budget was agreed and an outside contractor brought in. Within a matter of only two weeks the area was ready to be used by the children.

The children found it a special place to be and although relatively small in size it was very useful in supporting their learning and development. It was agreed that a maximum of ten children would be allowed to access the area at any one time.

Some months later I asked the head and the Year 1 teacher what the impact of the project had been. The feedback was that it had made a real difference:

(a) The indoor classroom was at times a much quieter place and general behaviour had improved significantly, particularly with some of the boys.

(b) Children were able to independently engage in activities – although at times the teacher or the teaching assistant were supporting/leading/modelling activities.

(c) Outcomes had significantly improved in a number of areas, including in mathematics and writing.

(d) The space was extremely popular with children who clearly wanted to be there.

(e) The emotional well-being of children was supported by the project and it actually improved the overall attendance in the class.

Outdoor Risk Assessment Pro-Forma

Name of Setting _____

Name/Role of person
completing the assesment _____

Reason for assessment _____

Date _____ Activity/Area _____

Hazards identified	Existing control measures in place
1	A
2	B
3	C
4	D
5	E

Who may be/has been harmed?	Assessment of residual risk (circle as appropriate)
1	
2	
3	High Medium Low
4	
5	

Further action required (if any)*

1

2

3

4

*NB: Where there are adequate control measures in place the activity/areas will be at low risk.
Where there are insufficient control measures in place the risk may well be higher.*

STEP BY STEP GUIDE TO DEVELOPING YOUR OUTDOOR AREA

Step 1

Share your ideas and the concept

- Involve as many people in your team as possible and parents/carers of children attending.

- Think about the potential benefits of developing your outdoor space and how it will support improved outcomes.

- Be positive and enthusiastic and try to include everyone and their ideas.

Step 2

Set up a team to manage the project

- Include representatives from all groups of people: staff, parents, community and governors/management committee.

- Think about how you will communicate information to all groups and how often.

- Be aware that the lack of a structured management group is often the main cause of project failure.

Step 3

Survey your site

- Get hold of a good quality, scaled-base plan or draw up your own.

- Look at two main aspects: 1) Physical features such as access routes, boundaries, services, hedges, trees and fences etc. 2) Current use such as when it is used and by whom.

- Collate attitudes and opinions about the grounds from staff and children.

Step 4

Identify your children's needs

- Use existing data on achievements and any gaps that need to be provided for across groups of children.

- Concentrate on what children 'need' rather than what you would want or like.

- Ask adults and children what they would like to do in the grounds.

- Consult the revised Early Learning Goals and Development Matters.

Step 5

Create a vision/development plan

- Use steps 1 to 4 to create a statement of intent i.e. your vision for the outdoor space/s.

- Using your base plan, outline the areas in which various uses have been identified (both current and potential).

- Bear in mind this will be a zoning plan and will show the general overall structure of future use. It should help iron out any conflicts that might develop.

- It may be appropriate here to prioritise if a lot of changes appear necessary.

- Seek quotations for any proposed work from outside contractors. (Ideally get three quotes so you can compare them.)

Playing and Learning Outdoors © Terry Gould. Published by Featherstone 2013

Step 6

Identify solutions to any potential problems

- If all the guidance is followed from all of the previous stages, this can be approached with confidence!

- The easiest changes to implement are organisational i.e. those involving training, renovating existing resources or features and purchasing or acquiring small pieces of equipment.

- Larger changes may include/require design solutions and engaging an outside contractor.

Step 7

Implement changes

- Divide up any work to be done and use skills within your group.

- Draw up an 'Action Plan' setting out a timetable of events. This plan, along with your 'Vision Plan', will be useful to send along with application forms to any potential funding sources.

- Think about long term maintenance and management implications.

- Implement physical changes - this can be done by on outside contractor or others.

- Award any contracts at this stage. (Ensure you visit some of their previous work to check quality.)

Step 8

Monitor and evaluate changes

- This is a useful tool for feedback or publicity and also helps to demonstrate the changes that have been brought about. (People soon forget how it used to be!)

- Evidence also helps if you need to attract any further funding.

- You may notice changes in the following areas: behaviour, accidents, attainment, time spent outside by staff and children.

- Include collating and displaying parents and children's attitudes towards the changes made to your outdoor space/s grounds.

- This evidence is also useful to show Ofsted when they visit.

Playing and Learning Outdoors © Terry Gould. Published by Featherstone 2013

Evaluation of Effective Outdoor Practice

A focus on good practice outdoors: organisation and management	Fully provided	Partly provided	Planned to be provided	Not in place
Do children have the opportunity outdoors to:				
Engage in cross-curricular activities and experiences?				
Independently select materials/equipment to develop and extend their play?				
Go outdoors in all weathers?				
Be independent in their play/activities, choosing some of the activities they engage with?				
Negotiate and engage in shared discussion with adults and other children?				
Engage in both adult-led and child-initiated activities including group/circle time and focused activities?				

Playing and Learning Outdoors © Terry Gould. Published by Featherstone 2013

Evaluation of Effective Outdoor Practice (contd.)

A focus on good practice outdoors: organisation and management	Fully provided	Partly provided	Planned to be provided	Not in place
Do adults:				
Offer some continuous provision outdoor learning opportunities?				
Provide a range of portable and fixed resources/equipment, which are open ended?				
Plan and provide for outdoor learning opportunities across all seven areas of learning?				
Respond to children's individual needs and interests?				
Observe independent and child-initiated activities resulting in appropriate intervention and future planning?				
Observe and assess children's progress?				
Use appropriate questioning and suggesting to extend children's ideas and thinking skills?				
Share with parents/carers the importance of outdoor learning?				
Allow children sufficient time outdoors to become engrossed and provide the space they need for their activities?				
Ensure that there are policies and procedures, including risk assessments, in place for using the outdoor environment?				
Ensure that the outdoor environment offers sufficient challenges for all children across all areas of learning?				
Ensure that experiences outdoors are bigger, bolder, messier and noisier than those indoors?				

Evaluation of Outdoor Provision

Nature of experience/s offered by / planned to be offered by setting	Details on resources provided / planned to be provided
Kick, roll, bounce, throw, aim and catch using: balls, beanbags, quoits and other small equipment	
Jump, hop, run, move and dance	
Balance and crawl	
Climb and swing	
Manoeuvre, pull, push and pedal a range of wheeled vehicles	
Make dens	
Engage in imaginative role play including dressing up	
Plant and grow a variety of plants, vegetables and flowers	
Explore and experiment with a range of natural materials including sand and water	
Problem solve through a range of activities	
Sit, read and gather with adults and other children	
Engage in large scale painting, drawing and model–making	

Playing and Learning Outdoors © Terry Gould. Published by Featherstone 2013

Evaluation of Outdoor Provision (contd.)

Nature of experience/s offered by / planned to be offered by setting	Details on resources provided / planned to be provided
Engage in writing/mark–making	
Observe and enjoy wildlife	
Explore and experiment with a range of natural materials	
Hide and be quiet	
Engage in large scale design and construction	
Explore making sounds using a range of materials and equipment	
Engage in sensory activities using plants, materials and resources	
Use a range of appropriate tools	
Investigate, experiment and explore	
Create and recreate patterns	
Engage in Maths and language–based games /activities	
Use ICT outdoors	

Playing and Learning Outdoors © Terry Gould. Published by Featherstone 2013

Bibliography and further reading

Bilton H. (2005) *Playing Outside* Routledge

DfES (2003) *Every Child Matters*

Gould T. (2011) *The Fabulous Foundation Stage* Featherstone, an imprint of Bloomsbury

Gould T. (2011) *Effective Practice in Outdoor Learning* Featherstone, an imprint of Bloomsbury

Isaacs S. (1932) *The Children We Teach* University of London Press

Keeler R. (2008) *Natural Playscapes — Creating Outdoor Environments for the Soul* Exchange Press

MacMillan M. (2009) *The Nursery School* BiblioBazaar

Ouvry M. (2003) *Exercising muscles and minds* National Children's Bureau

Staggs L. (2001) *Effective Practice In Reception Classes* Conference Manchester

Roberts A. (2011) *The Little Book of Mini Beast Hotels* Featherstone, an imprint of Bloomsbury

Stock-Kranowitz C. (2005) *The Out Of Sync Child—Reorganising and Coping with Sensory Processing Disorder* Skylight Press

Vygotsky L. (1978) *Mind in society — The Development of Higher Psychological Processes* Harvard University Press

Wells G. (1985) *The Meaning Makers: Children Learning Language and Using Language to Learn* Heinemann Educational Publishers

White J. (2007) *Playing and learning outdoors* Routledge

White J. (2009) *Outdoor provision for very young children* Early Years Update, Issue 66, March 2009 pages 8–10

Willshaw M. (20 June, 2013) HMCI Speech at Church House Westminster